IN SEARCH OF VIKINGS

MARIE SUTTON

First published 2020

Text and illustrations copyright © Marie Sutton

Typesetting and layout by Tim Wakeling

Thank you so much, Tim, for your command of the English language and your amazing IT skills, without which our project would be lost in a drawer somewhere.

ISBN: 9798580895963

To our wonderful children Rosemary and Ben

May their lives never stop being an adventure and may peace always be their guide.

THE CREW OF THE NANTUCKET TRADER

Arthur Sutton - *Captain*

Marie Sutton - *First Mate & Cook*

Rosemary - *Able Seaman*

Ben - *Able Seaman*

CONTENTS

Coffee and memories	9
Aberdovey	11
Back to the beginning	13
Disaster or Cream Teas	18
Scotland, Here We Come	22
Tow-paths, Bikes and a Gunship	25
Nessie or What?	28
Visitors and Waves	33
Land Ahoy	36
Canals and Lakes Galore	39
Island Hopping	46
Midnight Anchorage	48
Shattered Peace	52

COFFEE AND MEMORIES

Wind sighing through the pine trees
Seagulls screaming overhead
On looking up I see a majestic white-tailed sea eagle
Weaving and ducking to avoid sharp beaks of those angry gulls

This morning, the lure of good westerly winds have led lots of sailboats out to play on the waves between a myriad of islands, ready to explore new bays and coast for barbecues on the rocks with family and friends.

A swan family paddle up to us: Mum, Dad and four signets, the sun reflecting them in dancing motion in the morning-coloured sea.

On the shore, the pine tree roots hide a sandy track within. Mmm ... a mystery. Whose home is this?

A ferry boat steams past our entrance carrying shoppers and holidaymakers back to mainland Dalarö.

While I'm sitting on deck enjoying these sights, Arthur is down in the saloon writing the ship's log of the journey from the Finnish Archipelago.

Leaving Utö, the last lighthouse island of Finland, we motored (no wind) south west to Sandhamn, the lighthouse island that welcomed us into the Stockholm Archipelago, Sweden. By the time we had reached this haven on Ornö (which means Eagle Island), we had travelled non-stop for twenty four hours.

We nestled down to a well-earned sleep before the occupants of the moored boats were astir and the first morning bathers splashed in the cool refreshing water.

Over the last few days, as we have been enjoying this quiet natural harbour, memories of our first adventure on the Nantucket Trader slipped into focus...

ABERDOVEY, MAY 1996

Snuggled inside the harbour at Aberdovey on a warm sunny day, Rosemary and Ben were busy with school friends who had come with Mr. Cummins, their head teacher from Christleton Primary school, to help us prepare for our epic journey.

"How many tins of baked beans?" asked Michael with a marker pen at the ready.

"Two hundred", replied Ben with a smile. "It's in case I don't like some of the other food."

Laughter erupted over the wheelhouse roof. Four friends with Rosemary and Ben were sorting and coding tins: for example, 'BB' for 'baked beans', before their labels were discarded and passed through the hatch to be stored under the bunks in the saloon.

Arthur was busy up the mast fitting a new radar, an important bit of kit that enables us to see other boats when it's nasty or foggy.

A little boy stood transfixed on the quayside looking down at all the activity on the wheelhouse roof. The tide was out and Nantucket sat on the sand, leaning against the harbour wall.

"Dad," the boy said, tugging at his Dad's sleeve, "Is it a pirate ship?"

I overheard and smiled.

"She's preparing for an adventure into the little-known waters of the Northern Seas from where the Vikings and Norsemen came and plundered our shores many years ago, so we must be prepared. Who knows what may lie before us?"

BACK TO THE BEGINNING

Truth be told, we had already had more than enough adventure just getting to Wales.

Nantucket Trader's mooring was in the local fisherman's harbour of St. Helier, in Jersey. She had previously had twenty-four years adventuring with crews of eight plus a skipper in the Channel Islands, across to the French coast and down the Atlantic to the Canary Islands, off the West Coast of Africa.

On Arthur's birthday on 27 March, friends had driven us and a whole load of stuff to Manchester Airport from Chester for our flight to the Channel Islands. John and Sonia, her previous owners, collected us from the tiny island airport and drove us, with our crazy amount of luggage, to St. Helier's harbour.

We saw Nantucket nonchalently leaning against the quayside wall, as is her wont when the tide is out, snuggled between the fishing boats. We had seen this rugby-ball-shaped schooner the year before, and with a family "Yes" we had purchased her, knowing she was the right boat for us.

The next few weeks kept us busy. Rosemary and Ben had chosen their top bunks opposite each other in the saloon and prepared to make it home.

Whispered voices were heard in the mornings as they checked to ask us in our aft cabin: "Is it time to get the croissants?"

Right at the beginning of the quay from the town was a little bakery selling fresh croissants and warm French bread. As they approached the deck, the smell of coffee wafted up the opened hatch and we contentedly sat in the cockpit delighting in our French breakfast.

A month later we were preparing to cross the English Channel to Plymouth to register the boat and make our way westward to Wales.

There was quite a lot of work getting the boat ready for sailing, during which time we explored Jersey, discovering some of her rich history and of course visiting the famous zoo.

We had welcomed our special friends, Sally and Lynn, for Easter and met some interesting people. Now it was time to move on.

Alan, a friend who had come to help, sailed with us on our maiden journey. Good job too, as I had my head in the bucket whilst still in view of Jersey. Also the auto-helm packed up, so dear Alan was a real Godsend, as an experienced sailor.

With Plymouth just a stone's throw away, we dropped anchor in the early morning light, in the first cove of the Cornish coast called Corsands. We rowed Alan ashore so he could catch a train back to the Midlands, and we snuggled down to sleep.

Suddenly the loud engines of a powerful rib boat slowed down as she approached us and asked to board us.

"Sure," we replied.

The Anti-Smuggling squad boarded with a gorgeous Spaniel dog. Rosemary and Ben were delighted as with waggy tail he sniffed around the boat. Afterwards, Arthur sat across the middle seat of the rib for a trip to Plymouth, an exciting ride and a painful departure of money to the tax man.

For a few days we explored this quaint seaside village and caught a ferry over to Plymouth, where Sir Francis Drake had played bowls whilst the Spanish Armada was in the English Channel ready to attack.

On leaving Corsands travelling westward, we sailed close to naval waters where live ammunition was exploding, and an official vessel came to check we weren't going any closer.

Nantucket was skipping along nicely with her main sail and the Genoa (front sail) billowing in the wind. We were nearing our assigned anchorage up the Helford River and preparing to bring the main sail down.

"Oh no," exclaimed Arthur, "It's stuck!"

Quickly he put on a safety harness and issued instructions to us all. Rosemary took the helm with Ben alongside and I stood on the wheelhouse roof to hold the safety line whilst Arthur climbed the forty foot mast.

He seemed an age. The sail didn't want to part with the mast track and the waves sent the mast, with Arthur hanging on, first one side then the other over the sea.

Finally with job done and the sail safely tied to the boom, Arthur motored us into Helford River, safe out of the building wind and sea's swell. Of course I did the truly English thing whenever stressful situations come our way: made a cup of tea.

That evening the winds increased so I suggested that we go ashore for a walk. Arthur wasn't really keen to leave the boat but as the family had managed well, thought "a change is as good as a rest".

So with dinghy over the side, we clambered in and motored to a tiny hamlet and explored some of the oak and pine wooded coastal path.

After our walk, the winds had increased even more, and as we approached Nantucket she was rocking from side to side. We just couldn't board; either she would come crashing down on top of us or fling us over the other side of the boat.

We turned round and found a small cottage on the shore. The lady there allowed us to leave the dinghy in her garden. She had no room to put us up but she kindly walked with us up to her friend's B&B.

The room was pretty, cosy, and warm. We were cold, hungry, wet (oh, by the way, it was pouring down), and somewhat nervous. Tentatively I asked whether we could have some water. Well, the lovely lady came up to the room with a tray of steaming tomato soup and a plate of scones. Oh, heaven!

We took it in turns to have hot, relaxing, not to mention cleansing, showers. Bliss. Then we snuggled into our beds, turned the lights out and were soon sound asleep.

DISASTER OR CREAM TEAS

Next morning the storm had abated and we descended the stairs to the aroma of English cooked breakfast. "Eat everything," I whispered to Rosemary and Ben. Silly thing to say: everything was delicious.

With us all fully refreshed and a skip in our step, we followed the wooded cliff top path overlooking the bay, back to the cottage.

Looking down to the bay, I stopped in my tracks and exclaimed:

"Do you see what I see?"

Arthur, Rosemary and Ben all looked in the direction I was pointing.

"There's nothing, Mum."

"Yes, but that's the point. Nantucket should be there … and she isn't."

"Oh no!" gasped Arthur.

We hurried down the path to the hamlet where Arthur dived into the red phone box. He dialled the harbour authorities explaining that our boat is missing but the occupants are all safely ashore.

"OK," came the reply, "ring back in an hour and we'll tell you what we know."

Dejected and tearful, we knocked at the door of the cottage by the shore. The lady welcomed us in and, hearing our news, made us all a cup of tea – my answer to all stress. As we drank in tearful silence, she told us stories of how she'd seen sixty foot yachts break up in an hour on the rocks in front of her home. Ben began to cry.

"But it's our home!"

Arthur returned to the phone box, and fifteen minutes later we were motoring in our dinghy to reclaim Nantucket.

The harbour master had explained to Arthur, "It's OK, she's hooked herself onto a visitors mooring up the Helford river. If you unhook her and take her further up the river there's a larger mooring buoy. You'll be safe there and I'll see you at five o'clock."

As we made our way upstream, it became clear what had happened. With the storm winds she had dragged her anchor, mysteriously and wonderfully skirting round the boat-eating rocks, and slipped between very expensive large yachts. Finally she had hooked herself on to a visitors mooring buoy, with a smile, as if to say "What took you so long?"

A local ferryman called out as I was pulling the anchor chain in: "Think you will have lost your anchor".

"Oh," I said, smiling as I unhooked it off the mooring line.

At five o'clock, the harbour master motored over to our new anchorage. Laughing and pointing to the sky, he exclaimed: "I think someone is looking after you."

In unison we replied: "We think he is", laughed and had another cup of tea.

We had a few days recovering, with picnics in sunny spots up the river, and as we relaxed, we remembered previous happy holidays camping here with our caravan and miracle dinghy. On one such holiday we had visited the seal sanctuary for a hot, sunny, fun day. Rosemary brought a cuddly seal and Ben, being Ben, brought a shark. They now lived on Nantucket in their respective berths, where occasional misdemeanours from Mr. Shark would be followed by screams from Rosemary: "Don't you dare eat my seal!"

With peace all aboard, we set off to sail round Cornwall's rocky tip at Land's End.

As night drew on, the winds increased to gale force. Poor Arthur struggled to keep the boat on course and well away from the wreck-infested waters of the north Cornish coastline.

First light saw us in calm waters following marker buoys into a cove at Milford Haven, south west Wales. At last - peace and quiet after the noise and strain of the storm!

(Rosemary had amazingly slept soundly through it all, totally oblivious as she snuggled under the stairs in the saloon.)

Winds were light as we next rounded the Pembroke coast, and we were thrilled to see puffins bobbing happily on the gentle waves. They really are much smaller than we imagined.

The night was perfectly still and the stars just stunning, as we drifted, becalmed, in the waters of the Irish Sea, waiting for high tide to come over the bar into Dovey Estuary and Aberdovey harbour.

So now you see, we are up to our earlier chapter in Aberdovey.

Grandma lived in Tywyn, just five miles up the coast, where we had stored boat equipment, food, clothes and books, ready to stow on board. We enjoyed a happy reunion with my Mum, scrummy meals, and non-moving beds.

SCOTLAND, HERE WE COME

Time to continue north. With stores all safely housed we left Aberdovey quay with waving, well-wishing friends, cheering us on with "Bon Voyage".

Grandma said her goodbyes from home. "It will be too sad to see you go," she said.

This part of our journey was to take us up to Scotland via the Irish Sea through the Crinan Locks and on through the magnificent West Coast to Fort William. Frank, another good sailing friend from Tywyn, offered to go with us. Of course we were delighted; especially as I'd already spent so much time with my head in the bucket.

My most favourite watch on the helm was the four a.m. morning watch. The beauty of the early sunrise, and the small blue dolphins playing between the stern and the bows, helped keep me awake.

Our first anchorage after sailing past the Isle of Man was Campbell Town on the Isle of Mull. After tea our evening entertainment was watching the diving Gannets fishing so elegantly for their supper.

The next day we sailed between the Isles of Mull and Arran: quite a spectacle with the Arran Mountains rising tall on our starboard side. By late afternoon we motored into the Ardrishaig Basin, the beginning of our journey through the Crinan Canal. Frank sadly had to leave us to catch a train from Lochgilphead back to Tywyn for work. He'd been a great help and fun to have around.

The Crinan Canal was built by Thomas Telford, the famous engineer. It was opened in 1801 and meant boats no longer had to navigate the long and hazardous route around the Mull of Kintyre. Of course I loved the idea of a short cut, with the added bonus of showers and lovely towpaths for walks and bike rides. Together Rosemary, Ben and I learned how to operate the locks as we slowly motored through this gentle undulating landscape.

It was a beautiful sunny morning in Crinan Village as we waited for slack tide to venture out into the Sound of Jura. Even so, powerful whirlpool eddies

danced in circles all around us and Duntrune Castle looked impressive in the morning sun. We sailed up the Firth of Lorne, and soon were passing Oban. The morning sun picked out her whitewashed cottages, while fishing boats and ferries bobbed in her harbour.

The whole of this West Coast of Scotland was so beautiful. The landscape and wildlife kept us on deck just soaking up the sights as we travelled on into Loch Linne, past the narrow sound of Corran with its lighthouse and ferry crossing and on up to Fort William.

This area too was a place revisited from our caravan and dinghy days, when our toddlers redesigned loch shorelines, listened to stories of "Hairy Haggis", and enjoyed white-shelled beaches with crystal clear waters. We remembered a small ferry trip to a seal island on Loche Linne; so as we neared this same outcrop of rock, we slowed down to enjoy close-up views of seals and their pups basking in the sun and playing lazily in the sea.

Tow-paths, Bikes and a Gunship

Soon Fort William came into view, with the majestic mountain of Ben Nevis towering behind it. From here it was just a short hop to the Caledonian Canal.

We waited by the tar-soaked oak canal gates for the lock keeper to open them for us. Inside we entered a wide basin with the lock keeper's cottage, office, toilet and showers for visitors, with plenty of space to moor.

One of the doctors in Tywyn, on hearing we were going to Fort William, gave us a letter to pass on to the lock keeper. He had met him as a crew member of a yacht competing in the "Three Peaks Sailing Challenge". This race began in Barmouth, sailing to North Wales with a run up Snowdon, continuing sailing up to Cumbria and a run up Scafell Pike and finally sailing up the Scottish coast to Fort William, with a hard slog up the largest mountain of Britain, Ben Nevis. Too much like hard work for us. But we duly handed over the letter to a surprised lock keeper, as we introduced ourselves.

We chose to moor a little way into the canal by a landing stage and settled down here for a couple of weeks as Arthur had work to do on the boat. It was a great place to ride bikes up and down the towpaths, take evening walks, and go on bus excursions to Fort William and the swimming pool, where amazingly we met some people we knew from Aberdovey. Small world!

Well, this canal was also built by Thomas Telford, this time to save sailors from having to navigate the heavy seas off the north coast of Scotland. We watched all shapes and sizes of boats pass by, some on their journey to Inverness on the east coast; others arriving here from Inverness; and some just holidaying in one of the beautiful lochs.

On one occasion, we were excited to see a Danish gun boat moored in the basin. The sailors seemed very friendly, so I asked a lady sailor whether we could have a tour on board, explaining that we were home schooling and it would be very interesting.

"Umm ... well, I can ask."

She came back shortly after with a smile and said she could show us around, but no cameras. The sailor explained that she was a torpedo gunner and showed us which was her gun. In passing, she also mentioned that she was always sick at sea. That cheered me up as I explained that I often had my head in the bucket. Now after three years she had applied for a desk job in the Copenhagen naval base.

The next day we watched in amusement as this gun ship manoeuvered into the first lock. She was so tight. They pushed and pulled, and eventually managed to close the gates behind her, with the bows right into the V of the further gate.

NESSIE OR WHAT?

After our time in the Corpach basin, with jobs done, we were ready to discover the rest of the Caledonian Canal in the stunningly beautiful surroundings of the Great Glen, and on to Inverness.

We became pretty skilled in opening and closing lock gates, of which there were plenty in this hilly landscape, and enjoyed sailing on the lochs (lakes) of Lochy and Oich before reaching the Neptune Staircase. It had eight locks, and

was the longest staircase lock in the UK. Fortunately they were hydraulically operated, but there was still plenty of tying and untying of mooring lines to keep us busy. As you can imagine, we had got to know some of our fellow travellers that stopped and started at similar times on the journey.

When we birthed alongside the quay at Fort Augustus after our busy descent down the Neptune staircase, one sailor asked us if he could come aboard Nantucket. He was intrigued to know her story.

"Yes, of course," replied Arthur, "Welcome!"

With a cup of tea and cake, we shared Nantucket's history of being the last wooden boat built in Jersey. An architect had heard that the Nantucket trading ships from Newfoundland, mentioned in the classic book Moby Dick, had a reputation of not losing sailors overboard.

"Sounds good," he thought, and so he asked the Newfoundland Museum to send him the plans. Then in 1972, this two-thirds smaller scale Schooner was completed, built from mahogany planking on oak frames with afrimosa decking, designed inside as a skipper charter and registered in Jersey.

Our visitor in turn told us that he was one of the captains of "The Whale". We looked quizzically at him: "The Whale?"

He laughed.

"Yes, it's due to dock here this evening, and tomorrow I can take you round and introduce you to the owner."

"Wow, yes please!" came our excited reply.

Before bedtime we took a leisurely stroll along the shore to Loch Ness, clambering some rocks to have a better look up the Loch.

"What is it?" exclaimed Rosemary.

"Perhaps it's Nessie," piped up Ben.

Arthur smiled.

"Let's just wait and see."

As this apparition drew closer, all became clear.

"It's the Whale!"

Slowly she came to the quayside of St. Augustine, and we watched as she was securely fastened to her new mooring.

"Cor, it's big - it really is a whale!"

The next sunny morning, we waited for our new skipper friend to take us meet the owner, Tom McClean. He cordially welcomed us on board and began to explain why he had built a whale.

Tom was an outdoor pursuits fanatic who loved a challenge. Once, he had decided to row across the Atlantic in the smallest rowing boat. Then he thought he'd quite like to cross in a bottle from New York to Falmouth. Having successfully achieved these crazy feats of endurance, his next idea was to cross the Atlantic in a whale. The Whale was built in steel on the east coast of Scotland and now he was taking it on its maiden journey to Fort William. Having quickly shared his story, he excused himself and our skipper friend escorted us around the ship.

It made our day to see this unique 65-foot whale (who by the way was called Moby) on Loch Ness. It changed our perception of this intriguing place. Is the legend of Nessie real? Who knows, but the tale of the Whale certainly is!

We sailed along Loch Ness into the last stretch of locks to the Muirtown basin at Inverness. With local shops and the all-important nice warm showers, it was a great place to wait for the best time to venture out through the last sea lock into Moray Firth and on to the North Sea.

You remember me telling the little boy in Aberdovey that we were travelling north to where the Vikings hailed from?

Well, you'll never believe it: the Vikings came and moored alongside the quay just behind us. Our jaws dropped as we watched them arrive in their longboat ... honest, we did!

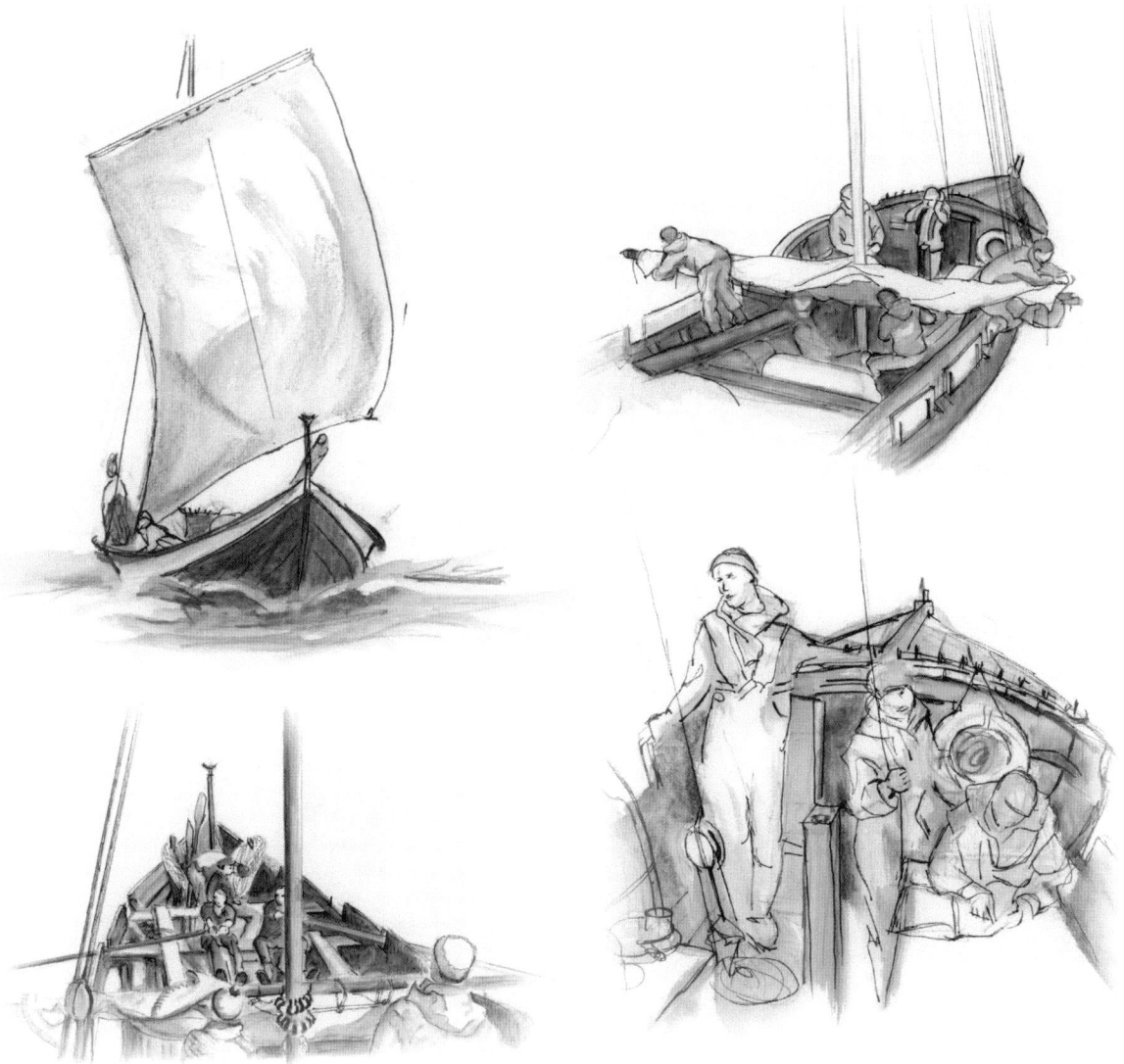

We helped them tie up, and of course just had to satisfy our curiosity. "Who are you? Where do you come from? And where are you going to?"

The good-natured Vikings shared their story.

They hailed from the ancient Norse fishing port of Bergen in Norway. This fine wooden vessel was the last fishing boat of this Viking style built there in the early 1900s.

Dressed in warm, traditional Norwegian jumpers, woolly hats and socks, and of course waterproofs, they'd sailed out of Bergen Fjords, across the North Sea to Shetland, across to Scotland's north coast and hugged the East coast down to Inverness (though maybe not unnoticed). They cooked on deck and slept sardine-like inside a wooden shelter in the stern, with a really long tiller reaching across the top.

As a conquering sea vessel of bygone days, it's easy to see why they were so successful in conquering our north-eastern shores. They had a gaff rigged sail, long oars and a very shallow draft which meant they could creep quietly, unseen, into estuaries and inlets.

This enthusiastic crew of six were on their way to Brest in France, to attend a wooden boats festival. They were travelling through the Caledonian Canal to the west coast of Scotland, along the Irish coast and finishing with a well-timed dash across the English Channel to Brittany on the north coast of France.

VISITORS AND WAVES

The next leg of our journey would take us to Gothenburg in Sweden, across the widest part of the North Sea, taking five days in all.

I must admit I was a little nervous with how well I'd fare, considering I had my head in the bucket so many times already, plus making meals for a hungry crew. Arthur was keeping an eagle eye on the weather forecasts. We were waiting for a period of settled weather with fair winds, enabling us to sail between Norway and Denmark through the Skaggerak Strait.

Meanwhile, we had chatted to a local fisherman who told us that the best time to see the dolphins in the Moray Firth was near high tide.

With a good weather forecast, the right winds and high tide, we passed through the last sea lock and out into the estuary that would eventually take us out into the North Sea.

We had already sailed a good way out from Inverness when squeals of delight erupted from Rosemary and Ben, as they pointed our gaze starboard.

There they were, leaping high into the air, twisting into a back flip and splashing back into the waves. It was so thrilling to watch the antics of these friendly creatures. In all we spotted three groups of dolphins as in turn they hooped through the waves to passing boats to play under the bow's wash.

We were not disappointed - they saw us and came tumbling through the waves to play between our boat and another sailboat leaving from Inverness, ducking under the bows. What a breathtaking and fabulous sight, really the best entertainment.

With sails set well, we sailed nicely with land gradually disappearing from view. Believe or not I didn't have my head in the bucket, but it was a strange feeling that we wouldn't see land for a few days.

On the second day out at sea we had a surprise visitor. A small, black bird, flew into the wheelhouse and perched on the chart table. We all snuck a view, trying not to frighten it, but it seemed totally exhausted. We left it some bread crumbs and water. After a day's free ride it was sufficiently refreshed to continue on its way. Ben checked in his bird book and we thought it was a storm petrol, probably a young one.

Our steady forecast decided to change itself. The winds changed direction and increased in strength, until between Norway and Denmark the waves became really huge, splashing right over the deck and wheelhouse. Just two waves were as long as the forty-foot length of Nantucket.

By this time we had the foremain sail set with the wind vane, which worked really well with the motor running, to speed us across to Sweden. Arthur and I hunkered down in the wheelhouse taking it in turns to watch for ships, while Rosemary and Ben were snuggled in the family berth happily reading.

Suddenly Ben shouted out, "Dad, water is coming up the sink in the heads!"

Arthur dashed down the steps into the saloon and to the heads (the bathroom), expecting to turn off the sea cock under the sink ... only to find that there wasn't one.

Back to the wheelhouse to pump out the bilges - but there was something blocking the pipe. Oops! We now had a saloon awash with orange, smelly, bilge water and dislodged items merrily floating on it: books, shoes, and sleeping bags.

LAND AHOY

Well, the good thing was that the combined sails and motor pushed us quicker towards Sweden, so we reached calm settled waters near Gothenburg in four days instead of five. It was a beautiful sunny morning that highlighted the large pyramid shaped marker and lighthouse, built on a rocky outcrop, which guided us into the Gothenburg Archipelago and eventual harbour.

Lots of little islands, with small sheltered harbours and pretty red houses, were dotted along the coast, and enormous towering container ships were docked along the north shore. As we continued under high bridges up the river along which Gothenburg was built, the city proper came into view, with large passenger ferries lined on its starboard shore.

We sailed up to the main town marina and found we were too wide to fit in, so we moored on the big quayside walls. The busy river traffic and the wash from the large Stena ferries did knock us around a bit.

So here we were in our first foreign port. Exhilarated and exhausted both, and glad to be moored safely. The saloon floor was cleaned up and we'd tidied sufficiently to live with, that'll do. We decided it was more important to explore this new city, so bikes were passed to shore and off we went.

We discovered Gothenburg loved cyclists. We had our own cycle paths with our own set of traffic lights, which made exploring the nearby city centre both fun and safe. Having picked up information and maps, we explored the city canal, parks, boulevards with their shops and even an art museum over the weekend.

Alongside the river, the quayside was wide and fun to cycle along with plenty to see. Large boats were moored here to change crew before continuing their journey or to simply explore the city like us. One of them was a tall ship called "Winston Churchill" flying the red ensign (British maritime flag). When we pulled up to take a look, Arthur surprised us by saying that he had sailed on her in the late 1960s. As the sailing fanatic at school, he'd won a scholarship to do a sail training tour of duty. Wow - we were well impressed.

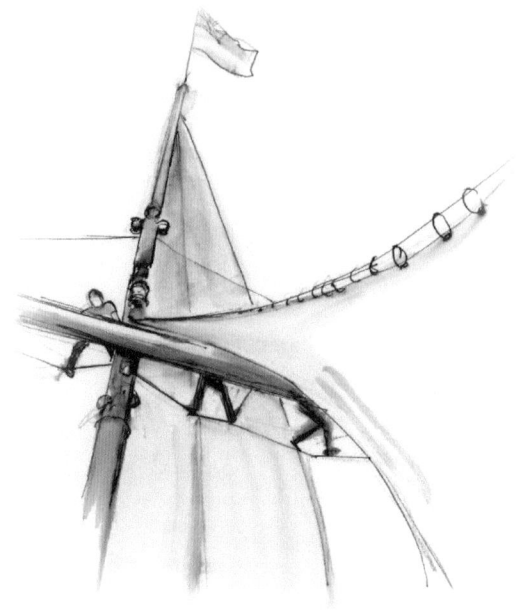

As one of the current crew were passing, I asked if we could have a look around, as Arthur had sailed on her all those years back. As we were shown around, Arthur shared stories of his exploits up the yard arm working the huge square sail and how comfortable it was to sleep in a hammock, though rather tricky getting in and out. Since his adventure on board this famous tall ship, Arthur had built his own sailing cruiser, named Maria, in his back garden in Chester. He moored her in Pwllheli and sailed the west coast of Britain and across to France in her.

During our traumatic North Sea crossing, the new auto helm Arthur had fitted in Scotland had just stopped working. On the Monday, as he was waiting for an expert to come to fix it, he found that a key had fallen out during our encounter with the big waves. So it was easily fixed and he cancelled the help. He also fixed the bilge pump. The culprit was a small curtain hook that had jammed in the pipe. We walked to the chandlers to purchase a sea cock for the sink, as well as charts for the Göta Canal and the east coast on the Baltic Sea.

CANALS AND LAKES GALORE

Back in Chester, a friend had kindly given us a gift to buy a ticket that would enable us to travel across Sweden to the Baltic via the Trollhätte ship canal, the large lakes and the Göta canal, instead of round the coast. So with the recent problems sorted, we prepared to discover Sweden.

We left the city behind us with its high bridges and lifting bridges with traffic lights to allow river traffic to pass underneath. Soon the countryside alongside the river was lush with farmland and forest, with pretty coloured wooden houses painted red, yellow or blue.

Eventually we came face to face with the huge steel gates of the Trollhätte ship canal in a deep rocky gorge - which was why the locks were needed.

There was a mooring pontoon where we waited for the traffic lights to turn green. We motored past these huge gates into a cavernous lock with twelve metre high walls. The big doors shut as we were trying to figure out how to ascend with ropes looped to ladders, as the waters rushed in to take us

#

frighteningly fast up these towering walls.

All hands on deck and plenty of confusion fending off Nantucket's bowsprit and stern alternately, watched by amused Swedish onlookers from the towpath above.

By the third lock we had finally mastered how to ascend the walls more smoothly. In the midst of all our activity, Ben suddenly piped up.

"Dad, are you supposed to have smoke coming out of the wheelhouse?"

"Oh no!" exclaimed a tired Dad. "The engine must have blown a gasket."

I muttered under my breath: "I've already blown mine."

The stress of the Trollhätte following on the heels of the North Sea crossing, proved too much for me and I became ill with shingles. We limped out of the canal to the side mooring to ask for help from the lock keeper.

Bo (a really Swedish name) was wonderful to us all as he rallied round, going out of his way to help us. He brought medicine for me, took Arthur to the importers to purchase a heat exchanger (it wasn't a gasket after all), and invited us to his home to meet his family. Rosemary and Ben bounced on the trampoline and raced round the garden in go carts with his children, followed by a scrummy meal. How kind was that! We felt so blessed.

As Arthur worked on the engine and I continued to rest, Rosemary and Ben explored the small hamlet of Trollhättan. Alongside the ship canal was a smaller one like the Caledonian, which was no longer in use. Its wooded towpaths provided plenty of exercise, finishing with a spectacular waterfall. It was also entertaining watching large cargo ships going up or down the three ship locks. Unlike us who swung all over the place, they filled the whole lock.

Once the engine was fixed and we had said bye to our new friends, we headed to Lake Vänern. It looked big on the chart, but as we entered it seemed even bigger - more like a sea. It was huge compared to any lake we had visited in the English Lake District or any of the Scottish lochs; in fact it is the largest lake in Sweden.

We set sail and headed north east past a town called Mariestad (my town) and on to Sjötorp, the beginning or end of the Göta Canal. Here we found out that the Göta Canal, as well as the old Trollhätte canal was designed by, yes you've guessed it, Thomas Telford, and built by Baltzar von Platen.

Arthur purchased the ticket needed to travel east on the canal, interspersed with lakes, to the Baltic Sea. We went through the first lock and found a good mooring place to explore this little town. The towpath was very popular with families and evening strollers. Several folk stopped and, pointing to our red ensign with its small Union flag in the corner, asked whether we were from the Bahamas, Australia or New Zealand. To each we patiently replied "No, just England".

One family didn't just walk away disappointed, but invited us for coffee the following day.

"Yes, we'd love to", came our united response.

When travelling through any new place, especially if it's a new country, it's always a joy to visit the homes of local people. Somehow it feels less "touristy", and we can share interesting stories about real lives. We sat in their garden with coffee and buns the next morning, chatting 'ten to the dozen' as my Mum used to say. Rosemary and Ben played with their little girl, easily picking up Swedish words.

The family offered us the use of their washing machine when they heard of the bilge water with sleeping bags and clothes floating in it. What another 'Godsend'. For two days, washing waved under the apple trees, clean and sweet-smelling.

On the second day of this marathon wash, Doug's family had a couple of friends visiting called Jan and Solveig. My face and neck were still pink from the calamine lotion to calm the shingles. Solveig noticed and asked what was wrong. I explained as best I could, not knowing Swedish names. Solveig said that she was a nurse working in Mariestad hospital, and that really I should have complete rest in a hospital for a couple of weeks. I laughed. "Not possible," I said.

Next morning, we heard a knock on the hull, and there were Jan and Solveig standing on the towpath. We welcomed them on board and made coffee.

"We have a week's holiday," Solveig explained. "We would love to come to help you through the Göta Canal - it'll be fun, and I can look after you, Marie."

"Wow," perked up Arthur. "Yes please, that would be wonderful."

Having said our goodbyes to Doug's family, thanking them for all their kindness, we welcomed Jan and Solveig on board the following morning. Bags were stowed in the saloon where they would sleep with Rosemary and Ben, who excitedly showed them the workings of the boat.

We left Sjötorp to discover this famous waterway cutting through this country of Viking legend, whose people so far had shown us hospitality and kindness.

Only once had we encountered the old spirit of the Vikings. During June and July the northern countries enjoy what is known as the midnight sun. Far up north, in the Arctic circle, the sun never sets and in Gothenberg the nights are very short.

Between two and three o'clock in the morning, I heard a boat engine pull up behind the stern of Nantucket with the sound of men's voices talking and laughing. I thought of waking Arthur, but he was sound asleep. Then as quickly as they had come, they motored into the stream of the river, clutching our life buoy with safety light. I watched helplessly through the port hole of the aft cabin thinking maybe the Viking raiders are still alive and well. But of course this one encounter was soon forgotten in the warmth of all the kindness we had received since then.

The Göta's locks were fully automated, but our happy crew of Rosemary, Ben, Jan and Solveig still had plenty to do handling the mooring lines as we navigated this waterway. Jan was tall and strong to pull Nantucket quickly to berth and explain to our fellow Swedish travellers to let us get safely tied up before coming alongside us. It was always a concern for Arthur because the propeller on our eighteen tons of boat sent her sideways when in reverse - so it definitely wouldn't have been good for small plastic boats to be in our way!

Our week passed far too quickly as we motored through the canal stretches, interspersed with small towns with lifting bridges, little hamlets, farmland and beautiful small lakes, as well as the larger Lake Vättern.

Jan pointed out an osprey to Arthur as they were chatting at the helm. Solveig had lived in South Africa, so we sang the two Swahili songs that we knew with her. After evening meals (yes, we did introduce them to baked beans), we explored our wide variety of new moorings. The 58 locks making up this beautiful waterway afforded plenty of opportunities for Rosemary and Ben to help following boats by taking their lines and earning a good wage in sweets. The famous lock staircase in Berg, overlooking the lake Roxen, in particular meant their sweet jar kept for foreign travel never became depleted. Smiles all round.

We passed the last town of Söderköping before mooring in the basin at Mem inside the last lock leading to the Baltic Sea. Here we said our sad farewells to our fellow sailors, who had given us so much help, fun and laughter, even buying ice creams as we waited for the locks to open. Rosemary and Ben cycled back with them along the towpath to Söderköping, where Jan and Solveig planned to catch a bus back home.

After a week of exploring, biking and frisbee, we were ready to sail north on the Baltic Sea. To be honest, it looked and felt more like an enormous lake. We realised this was because of the narrow entrance between Denmark and Sweden which caused the high tides of the North Sea to peter out to just half a metre up here and so was hardly noticeable at all.

ISLAND HOPPING

As we sailed between the mainland and islands, we found lovely little coves and inlets to snuggle into for the night. At one such anchorage, a friendly inquisitor pulled alongside, asking about our flag and where we were from. He then invited us for tea at his summer cottage on his family's private island.

He collected us in the late afternoon in his motor boat, whilst his wife laid out a scrumptious tea with strawberries and ice cream. Their children dried themselves after jumping and swimming off the jetty so they could join us. It was a very old log cabin built by his grandparents. Once two-storey, it had been divided into two single-storey cabins to accommodate the ever-growing family. It was very beautiful and full of Swedish tradition. Annoyingly, I'd left the camera back on board; graciously they allowed us to quickly call in again the next morning so I could click away, before heading up to Sandhamn.

On the way we enjoyed another new sight: dogs in life jackets. We thought it so funny at first, as of course dogs can swim. Since then we have realised it's really quite useful, as the jackets have handles to enable the owners to lift the dogs ashore or help to board. We called out to a lady canoeing in our wake to give her golden retriever an oar as he sat regally in the back seat enjoying the ride.

There was glorious sunshine as we approached the narrow passageway between the famous landmark of Sandhamn on our starboard side and the

island on the port side with its tall lookout tower. There were pretty boat houses on the shore as we approached the famous marina, which hosts sailing races from Stockholm to Gotland and the more infamous midsummer parties.

MIDNIGHT ANCHORAGE

Following the big sea markers out into the Baltic Sea proper, we waved bye bye to Sweden. From here we had a full day's sail to cross over to Helsinki, riding the big following waves like a big dipper at the fairground. Well, I must have found my sea legs at last: this was the second long sail (the other being the North Sea) that I had managed without having my head in the bucket.

It was after midnight that we followed leading lights into Helsinki's harbour. What a big day!

We were tired and the harbour area was very dark. Arthur decided to drop anchor in the shade of an island with castle-like buildings silhouetted against the night sky.

Just as we were settling down for a well-earned rest, a search light scanned across our decks and a voice shouted out something in Finnish. Groggy-eyed and surprised, we shouted back: "English!"

"We want to board," came the response.

"Oh … déjà vu," we thought.

"Welcome," we called back.

Rosemary and Ben, who had been asleep, peered round their curtains, as two officious-looking men in uniform clambered on board. We welcomed them with a cheery smile, explaining "we've just arrived".

A stern-faced older man spoke in Finnish, while the younger one translated: "We know, we followed you here. You should have reported to customs first, not just drop anchor anywhere."

"Oh," exclaimed a bemused Arthur; the children enjoying the show from their bunks. "We thought that being from Europe we didn't need to come to customs, like when we arrived in Sweden."

"Ei, no" replied the not-happy-faced border guard. Anyway, after a few more questions and our cheerful responses, they relaxed. Apologies accepted, they asked us to follow them to the customs dock while they kept the search light on to guide us.

Several hours later, with official work finally attended to, we headed into Helsinki city waterfront and moored alongside a large quay by the onion-shaped domes of the Russian Orthodox Church. The morning light over the city was glorious, and across from us at five o'clock the open market was a-bustle with stallholders setting up for the day's business.

Later on that sunny morning, the harbourmaster pulled up alongside us. He explained that this wasn't a good place for us to be, and kindly took us over to the fish market with permission to be moored there for five days free of charge.

"Thank you so much," we said. "Kiitos!"

The "Fish Market harbour" was actually a short stay, shoppers mooring for boats coming from the nearby islands, which just happened to be in front of the fish market building.

First things first: we bought doughnuts from the fish market and relaxed with coffee in the cockpit, watching the hive of activity all around us.

Looking towards the other market we had seen earlier, we saw a small quay where local people sold their produce such as fresh fish, shelling peas and home grown vegetables. To the right of this was a large quayside for visiting

tall sailing ships, like Baltic traders, to exchange crew or just enjoy visiting the city. Behind us were large ferries for Stockholm and Tallinn.

Time to explore the maze of trestle tables and stalls of the open market that we had seen being set up earlier, with all its colour and variety and bustle. Old ladies were knitting and selling socks, hats and mittens. Craftsmen were whittling small wooden sculptures and I bought a moose – the first of what is now quite a collection!

There were handmade crafts from Lapland with blue, red and yellow felt hats of the Lapis people, curly birch wooden mugs, reindeer skins and juniper-handled carving knives, which Arthur couldn't resist. Ben bought a tiny paper knife, and for Grandma we found some lovely felt slippers.

Bakery stalls sold all kinds of different breads: rye breads with rice, potatoes or honey, and flat round rye breads with a hole in the middle so they could hang in the kitchens. We tried some of these and also different cheeses.

Delicious smells wafted up from food stalls selling different traditional dishes. Feeling rather hot and weary, we sat down on the quayside enjoying ice creams and laughing at the antics of seagulls stealing titbits from snacking families.

SHATTERED PEACE

After five fun-filled days exploring this vibrant city by foot and bike, we moved up to the N.J.K. sailing club, sitting proudly on its own island, with a little ferry going back and forth to the mainland.

Settling happily on a visitors' pontoon, still in sight of the market waterfront, we explored the tiny island and enjoyed our first sauna – a Finnish institution not to be missed, at least for me and Rosemary. The boys were not so enamoured.

After tea we relaxed for the evening with other boats from around the world. At nine o'clock on this first night, a loud bang rocked the peace and quiet.

"What on earth?!"

Running up on deck, we noticed smoke spiralling out of a small canon which stood on a plinth in front of the beautiful old building. That's how we discovered the practice of lowering the flag every evening. Boat owners stand by their flags ready to remove them for the night at nine o'clock, sharp. We smiled sheepishly at our neighbours and brought in the red ensign. Of course the next evening we were primed and ready. Since that time, sailing in the Finnish and Swedish Archipelagos, we have heard trumpets, bugles and trombones ring out "good night" at that time every evening.

A couple of weeks later, we moved to the HMV motorboat club in the north harbour behind the Russian Orthodox Church (you remember, the one with golden onions on its roof?). Between the marina and the Russian church was a harbour for traditional wooden sailing boats of all shapes and sizes, from large Baltic traders to small island boats, very similar to the Viking fishing boat we saw in Inverness.

Helsinki, like Gothenberg, had great cycle paths for safe and easy exploring. So we cycled over bridges and islands to the zoo island and saw our first snow leopard and reindeers.

Being in Helsinki was a golden opportunity to visit Tallinn. The capital of Estonia is famous for its old medieval city, and was loved by the Finns for cheaper shopping. So we jumped on our bikes really early one morning to catch a high speed ferry for our day trip.

Estonia had recently received independence from Russia, as the old Communism collapsed in 1991. On walking to the old town from the ferry terminal, we smiled at all the old Russian Lada taxis, pushed to one side with gleaming white new Opal taxis taking their place. The medieval town was undergoing a similar transformation with sounds of saws, hammers and drills resounding from courtyards and doorways.

Small quaint side streets and cobbled roads opened out onto squares with interesting shops and pavement cafes. Low arches revealed hidden courtyards encased in the towering outer walls of the old city. Alongside

these walls was an open market where I spotted some gorgeous Norwegian jumpers 'going for a song'. We so enjoyed experiencing this 'other world' and were glad of this opportunity to witness Tallinn's early days of transformation.

It's always fun when we see the red or blue ensign flying off the sterns of visiting boats from Britain, and back in the HMV club we chatted to the occupants of one such boat. The owner was English, his wife was French and their friend was from the USA.

They came aboard for a cup of real English tea and began the usual sharing of stories. The American explained the meaning of 'Nantucket'. It's an old Native American Indian harbour off the coast of Newfoundland, and its name means 'Haven of Peace'.

"Wow, that's wonderful!" we responded.

Now, twenty-one years later, it has undergone complete restoration by us and so is even more like its namesake. We pray that when folk sail with us, they too can experience our 'Haven of Peace'.

Printed in Great Britain
by Amazon